Explore
EUROPE

Molly Aloian & Bobbie Kalman

Crabtree Publishing Company

www.crabtreebooks.com

A Bobbie Kalman Book

Dedicated by Katherine Berti
Mojemu kochanemu ojcu chrzestnemu,
Wujkowi Wieskowi Murawskiemu.

Editor-in-Chief
Bobbie Kalman

Writing team
Molly Aloian
Bobbie Kalman

Substantive editor
Kathryn Smithyman

Editors
Michael Hodge
Kelley MacAulay

Photo research
Crystal Sikkens

Design
Katherine Berti

Production coordinator
Heather Fitzpatrick

Prepress technician
Nancy Johnson

Consultant
Dr. John Agnew, Professor,
UCLA Department of Geography

Illustrations
Barbara Bedell: pages 4 (bird), 20 (plant)
Katherine Berti: pages 4 (map), 7, 13, 21, 22, 26, 30, 31
Robert MacGregor: front cover (map), back cover (map), pages 8-9,
    12 (map), 14, 16, 18 (map), 20 (map)
Bonna Rouse: pages 12 (lily pad), 18 (tree), 25
Margaret Amy Salter: pages 4 (butterfly), 10, 17

Photographs
© Bryan & Cherry Alexander/Arcticphoto.com: page 19 (bottom)
BigStockPhoto.com: © Paul Maydikov: back cover; © Tyler Olson: page 22
Dreamstime.com: Edyta Pawlowska: page 24; Rui Vale de sousa:
    page 11 (bottom)
iStockphoto.com: front cover, pages 1, 10, 11 (top), 13, 14, 15, 16, 17, 18,
    19 (top), 20-21 (top), 23, 25, 27, 28, 29, 31 (top)
© ShutterStock.com: page 31 (bottom)
Other images by Corel, Digital Stock, and Photodisc

Library and Archives Canada Cataloguing in Publication

Aloian, Molly
    Explore Europe / Molly Aloian & Bobbie Kalman.

(Explore the continents)
Includes index.
ISBN 978-0-7787-3074-3 (bound)
ISBN 978-0-7787-3088-0 (pbk.)

    1. Europe--Geography--Juvenile literature.
I. Kalman, Bobbie, 1947- II. Title. III. Series.

D1051.A46 2007   j914   C2007-900735-X

Library of Congress Cataloging-in-Publication Data

Aloian, Molly.
    Explore Europe / Molly Aloian & Bobbie Kalman.
        p. cm. -- (Explore the continents)
    Includes index.
    ISBN-13: 978-0-7787-3074-3 (lib. binding)
    ISBN-10: 0-7787-3074-3 (lib. binding)
    ISBN-13: 978-0-7787-3088-0 (pbk.)
    ISBN-10: 0-7787-3088-3 (pbk.)
    1. Europe--Juvenile literature. 2. Europe--Geography--Juvenile
literature. I. Kalman, Bobbie. II. Title. III. Series.
    D1051.A56 2007
    914--dc22

                                                                    2007003498

Crabtree Publishing Company

Printed in the USA/082010/LG20100604

www.crabtreebooks.com   1-800-387-7650

Published in Canada
Crabtree Publishing
616 Welland Ave.
St. Catharines, Ontario
L2M 5V6

Published in the United States
Crabtree Publishing
PMB 59051
350 Fifth Avenue, 59th Floor
New York, New York 10118

Published in the United Kingdom
Crabtree Publishing
Maritime House
Basin Road North, Hove
BN41 1WR

Published in Australia
Crabtree Publishing
386 Mt. Alexander Rd.
Ascot Vale (Melbourne)
VIC 3032

Contents

Five oceans, seven continents	4
Learn about Europe	6
Looking at Earth	8
Weather in Europe	10
Water in Europe	12
Peninsulas and islands	14
Tall mountains	16
Many forests	18
Flat tundra	20
Urban areas	22
Villages and towns	24
Selling resources	26
Culture in Europe	28
Things to see and do	30
Glossary and Index	32

Five oceans, seven continents

There is water covering about three-quarters of Earth. The blue areas on the map below show where water is on Earth. The largest areas of water are called **oceans**.

ARCTIC OCEAN

EUROPE

ASIA

NORTH AMERICA

ATLANTIC OCEAN

PACIFIC OCEAN

AFRICA

PACIFIC OCEAN

SOUTH AMERICA

INDIAN OCEAN

AUSTRALIA / OCEANIA

SOUTHERN OCEAN

ANTARCTICA

Oceans on Earth

There are five oceans on Earth. From largest to smallest, they are the Pacific Ocean, the Atlantic Ocean, the Indian Ocean, the Southern Ocean, and the Arctic Ocean.

Ocean waters touch parts of Europe.

Continents on Earth

The five oceans flow around huge areas of land. These areas of land are called **continents**. There are seven continents. From largest to smallest, they are Asia, Africa, North America, South America, Antarctica, Europe, and Australia/Oceania.

Learn about Europe

This book is about the continent of Europe. There are 46 **countries** in Europe. A country is a part of a continent that has **borders** and a **government**. A border is the place where a country ends. A government is a group of people who are in charge of a country.

The continent of Europe is just a little bigger than the country of the United States.

Finding the countries

This box lists the names of many countries in Europe. The list is numbered. The numbers on the map show where these countries are in Europe.

1. SWITZERLAND
2. AUSTRIA
3. SLOVENIA
4. CROATIA
5. BOSNIA AND HERZEGOVINA
6. MONTENEGRO
7. ALBANIA
8. MACEDONIA
9. SERBIA
10. HUNGARY
11. SLOVAKIA
12. CZECH REPUBLIC
13. GERMANY
14. POLAND
15. UKRAINE
16. MOLDOVA
17. ROMANIA
18. BULGARIA
19. TURKEY-IN-EUROPE
20. BELARUS
21. LITHUANIA
22. LATVIA
23. ESTONIA

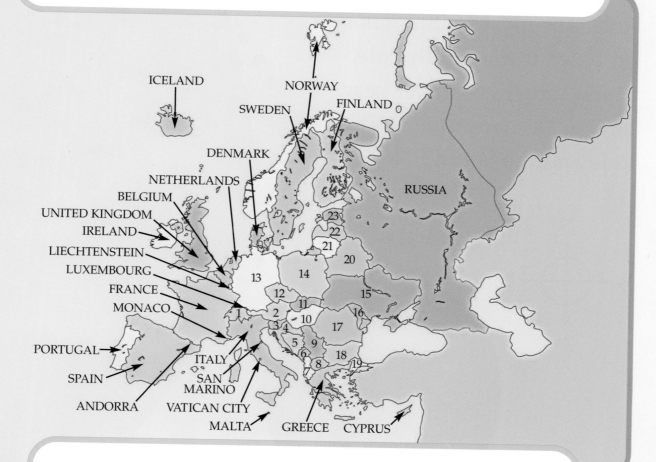

Fast fact

Europe is joined to the continent of Asia. The red line on this map marks the division between Europe and Asia. Part of Russia is in Europe and part of it is in Asia.

Looking at Earth

North, south, east, and west are the four main **directions** on Earth. The most northern point on Earth is the **North Pole**. The most southern point on Earth is the **South Pole**. The weather is cold all year long in areas near the North Pole and the South Pole.

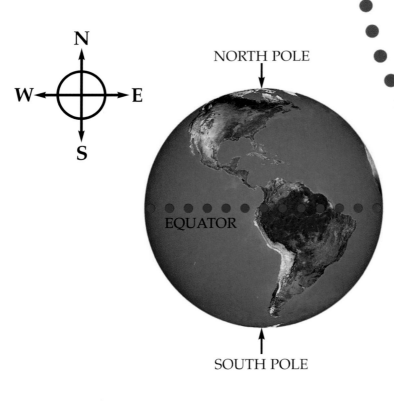

N
W E
S

NORTH POLE

EQUATOR

SOUTH POLE

EUROPE

North of the equator

The **Northern Hemisphere** is the part of Earth that is north of the **equator**. It is between the equator and the North Pole. Europe is in the Northern Hemisphere.

The equator

The equator is a circle that divides Earth into two equal parts. The weather is hot year round in places near the equator.

EQUATOR

South of the equator

The **Southern Hemisphere** is the part of Earth that is south of the equator. It is between the equator and the South Pole.

Weather in Europe

Climate is the long-term weather in an area. Climate is made up of temperature, rainfall, and wind. Different parts of Europe have different climates. The northern part of Europe is far from the equator. This area has a cold, windy climate. The parts of southern Europe that are closest to the equator have hot, sunny climates.

Sweden is in the northern part of Europe. It is far from the equator. It has a cold climate.

Fast fact
The United Kingdom is known for its rainy climate.

Dry or rainy

Some southern areas of Europe receive less than ten inches (25 cm) of rain each year. These parts of Europe have dry climates. Some northern areas of Europe receive a lot of rain each year. These parts of Europe have rainy climates.

Parts of Spain have dry climates. This picture shows a dry area in Spain.

Water in Europe

The Atlantic Ocean is along the west **coast** of Europe. A coast is land along an ocean or a **sea**. A sea is an area of an ocean with land around it. Parts of Europe's coasts are along seas. Some of the seas in Europe are the Adriatic Sea, the Baltic Sea, the Black Sea, and the Mediterranean Sea.

*There are many **rivers** in Europe. A river is a large area of water that flows into another waterway, such as a sea. The blue lines on this map show some rivers in Europe.*

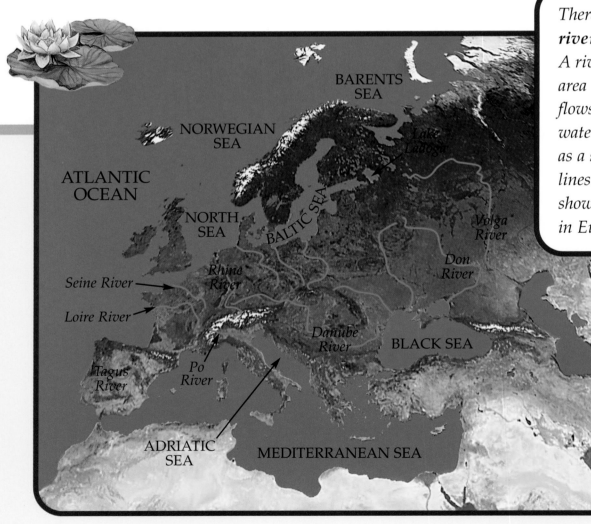

BARENTS SEA

NORWEGIAN SEA

Lake Ladoga

ATLANTIC OCEAN

NORTH SEA

BALTIC SEA

Volga River

Rhine River

Seine River

Don River

Loire River

Danube River

BLACK SEA

Tagus River

Po River

ADRIATIC SEA

MEDITERRANEAN SEA

Lake Ladoga

The largest **lake** in Europe is called Lake Ladoga. It is more than 124 miles (200 km) long. It is in the northwestern part of Russia, near Russia's border with the country of Finland.

Fast fact

Many people catch fish in Europe's waterways. People also **transport**, or move, goods on these waterways. They use boats and ships to transport goods from place to place.

*The Danube is the second-longest river in Europe. This part of the Danube is flowing through a city called Budapest. Budapest is the **capital** of Hungary.*

Peninsulas and islands

There are **peninsulas** in Europe. A peninsula is an area of land that sticks out into water. The Balkan Peninsula and the Iberian Peninsula are two peninsulas in Europe.

IBERIAN PENINSULA

BALKAN PENINSULA

There are also many *islands* in Europe. An island is land that is surrounded by water. This island is called Dragon Island. It is part of Spain.

A volcanic island

Iceland is a **volcanic island**. A volcanic island is the top of an underwater **volcano**. It is above ocean water. A volcanic island forms when a volcano under an ocean **erupts**. To erupt means to explode. When a volcano erupts under an ocean, hot liquid rock called **lava** spills onto the bottom of the ocean. The lava cools and gets hard. After a volcano has erupted many times, the lava piles up. It piles up until it rises above the surface of the water and forms an island.

Tall mountains

There are groups of **mountains** in Europe. Groups of mountains are called **mountain ranges**. The Alps, the Apennines, the Pyrenees, and the Carpathian Mountains are some mountain ranges in Europe.

The brown areas on this map show where some of Europe's mountain ranges are.

mountain ranges

Ibexes live in the Alps in Europe. They also live in the Pyrenees and the Apennines.

Life in valleys

alpine marmot

The climate is very cold and windy on the tops of mountains. Few people and animals live high on mountaintops. The climate in **valleys** is not as cold as the climate is on the tops of mountains. Valleys are low areas of land between mountains. Animals such as alpine marmots live in valleys. People live in valleys, too.

These homes are in a valley in Switzerland.

Many forests

There are **forests** between cities and farms in Europe. Forests are areas where many trees grow. There are different kinds of forests in Europe. **Boreal forests** and **temperate forests** are two kinds of forests in Europe.

forests

Boreal forests

Boreal forests are found in the northern parts of Europe. These forests have mainly **coniferous trees**. Coniferous trees have cones and needle-shaped leaves. Elk, beavers, and brown bears are some of the animals that live in boreal forests.

Temperate forests

Temperate forests grow farther south than where boreal forests grow. Temperate forests are made up of coniferous trees and **broadleaved trees**. Broadleaved trees have wide, flat leaves. Deer, squirrels, birds, and many other animals live in temperate forests.

In autumn, the leaves of broadleaved trees change from green to yellow, red, or orange. They then fall off the trees.

The Sami people live in the boreal forests of Norway, Finland, and Sweden.

Flat tundra

There is an area of flat, frozen land in northern Europe. It is called the **tundra**. Winter lasts almost the whole year on the tundra. Summer is short and chilly. Some **nomadic people** live on the tundra. Nomadic people move from place to place looking for food to eat and water to drink.

tundra

This picture shows reindeer that live on the tundra in Europe. Reindeer are a type of deer.

Get a move on

Some tundra animals, such as caribou and arctic terns, **migrate**. To migrate means to move from one area to another for a certain period of time. These animals leave the tundra before winter begins and travel south, where the weather is warmer. Arctic terns migrate farther than any other animal. They travel from the tundra to the South Pole and back.

Urban areas

More than 700 million people live in Europe! Most European people live in **urban areas**. Urban areas are cities. Moscow, London, St. Petersburg, Paris, Berlin, Madrid, and Rome are seven of the largest cities in Europe.

This map shows some cities in Europe.

REYKJAVIK

OSLO

ST. PETERSBURG

MOSCOW

LONDON

BERLIN

MINSK

PARIS

WARSAW

KIEV

PRAGUE

MADRID

MILAN

BUDAPEST

BUCHAREST

ROME

ATHENS

A city called Prague is on the Vltava River.

Fast fact

Many urban areas are close to waterways such as rivers.

Old and beautiful

There are many beautiful castles, **cathedrals**, and **museums** in Europe's cities. People from all over the world come to see these **historic buildings**. Some of the buildings in Europe's urban areas are thousands of years old.

This picture shows one of Europe's most famous churches. It is called St. Peter's Basilica. This church is in Rome, Italy. St. Peter's Basilica is over 500 years old!

Villages and towns

Some people in Europe live in **rural areas**. A rural area is a place in the countryside, outside a city. This picture shows a **village** in Slovakia. A village is a group of houses and other buildings in a rural area. Some small **towns** are also in Europe's rural areas. A town is bigger than a village, but it is smaller than a city.

Beautiful flowers

Bulbs and beautiful flowers grow well in some of Europe's rural areas. Bulbs are the round underground parts of some plants. This picture shows rows and rows of tulips growing in a rural area in the Netherlands. The Netherlands is famous for its tulips!

Selling resources

Europe has many **natural resources**. A natural resource is a material that is found in nature, such as oil. People sell natural resources to make money. **Timber** is one of Europe's natural resources. Timber is wood that people use to build things. People cut down trees to make timber.

This map shows where some natural resources are found in Europe.

wine grapes

potatoes

wheat

timber

corn

oil

Wine from Europe

A lot of **wine** is made in Europe and then sold to other countries around the world. Wine is a drink made from grape juice. People from many countries enjoy wines made in France, Germany, and Italy.

*Farmers grow grapes in this **vineyard** in France. A vineyard is an area where grapevines are grown. Farmers sell the grapes to wine-makers, who use them to make wine.*

Culture in Europe

Culture is the beliefs, customs, and ways of life that a group of people share. People in Europe **express**, or show, their cultures by participating in events and creating art, music, and dances. Sports and games are also parts of many European cultures. These pages show some parts of European culture.

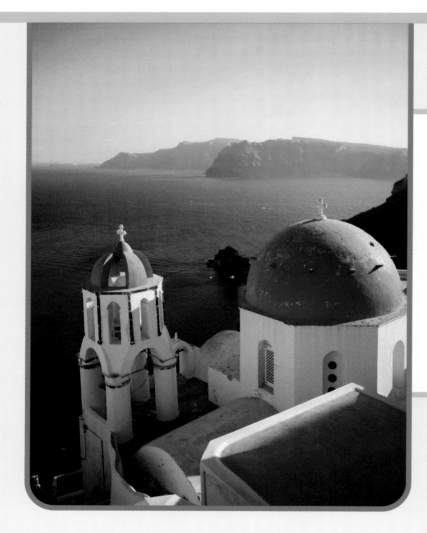

Artistic architecture

Architecture is a kind of art. It is the art of designing and making buildings. The kind of architecture in this picture is found in Greece.

Football fun

Many people in Europe enjoy playing and watching soccer games. In Europe, soccer is often called "football." There are many famous European football players.

Making music

Music is an important part of European culture. This picture shows a sculpture of a **composer** named Wolfgang Amadeus Mozart. He was born in Austria over 200 years ago. Many children today listen to the music of Mozart. His music is famous all over the world!

Things to see and do

People from all over the world visit Europe. They visit Europe for fun! People who visit places for fun are called **tourists**. These pages show just a few of the places that tourists visit. The maps show where the places are located in Europe.

*The Eiffel Tower is in Paris, France. It is 984 feet (300 m) tall and is made of **iron**. It was designed by a Frenchman named Alexandre Gustave Eiffel.*

*Many people visit Rome, Italy, to see a huge, old **amphitheater** called the coliseum. The coliseum is thousands of years old!*

The London Eye in London, England, is the largest ferris wheel in the world. It is 443 feet (135 m) tall! People who ride on the London Eye can see up to 24 miles (39 km) in all directions.

Glossary

Note: Boldfaced words that are defined in the text may not appear in the glossary.

amphitheater A building with a large main space where people watch and play sports

capital A large city where the government of a country is located

cathedral A large and important church

composer A person who writes music

historic buildings Buildings that are famous or important in history

iron A strong, hard metal

lake A large area of water surrounded by land

mountain A tall area of land with steep sides

museum A building where art and other objects are kept and displayed for people to see

nomadic people Groups of people who do not live in permanent houses and who travel from place to place to find food and water

volcano A mountain with an opening on its top; ash and hot lava sometimes erupt from the opening

Index

animals 17, 18, 19, 21
climate 10-11, 17
countries 6, 7, 13, 27
culture 28-29
forests 18-19
islands 14-15
lakes 12, 13
mountains 16-17
natural resources 26
oceans 4, 5, 12, 15
peninsulas 14
people 6, 13, 17, 19, 20, 22, 23, 24, 26, 27, 28, 29, 30, 31
rivers 12, 13, 22
rural areas 24, 25
tundra 20-21
urban areas 22, 23
valleys 17
villages 24
weather 8, 9, 10, 21